Notations on the Visible World

Notations on the Visible World

Copyright © Kathleen Wakefield 2000

All rights reserved under
International and Pan-American Copyright Conventions.

No portion of this book may be reproduced in any form without
the written permission of the publisher, except by a reviewer,
who may quote brief passages in connection with a review
for a magazine or newspaper.

Cover art
Milford Apetz – *Yellow Field*

Author photograph – David and Sharon Yates
Cover design, book design and production – Lynne Knight

For my family

Contents

Acknowledgments — ix

One

Grace Notes	3
You Have Been Exiled Here for a Reason	4
The White Slip	5
Some Nights	6
There and Back	7
Out of My Husband's Pockets	8
A Reply	10
I Was Lying in the Yard of the Methodist Church	11
Triptych	12
Botany	14
Judy,	15
Nocturne: Swift Water Point	16
Walking on Water	18
Translation	19
Desiring the Solicitude of Rain	20
Of Musick	22

Two

"You Shall Be Weeping and Crying"	25
When They Heard the Lord Calling	27
Remnants and Sudden Clarities	28
Angel of The Annunciation	29
Mary's Poem	30
Nativity	31
Meditation	32
Book of Names	33
After Looking at Bruegel	35
Reconsidering the Rift	36
Trying My Lines Aloud on the Back Porch	37
The Wild Boy Retreats to His Father's Truck	38
After a Time of Trouble	39
"The Third Heaven"	40

Bronze Woman	41
Granite Trail	42
August Latitudes	43
Banishment of the Alleluia	45
The Voice Outside	46

Three

The Swing	49
Cantata	50
Baptism of Christ	52
Agony in the Garden	54
Why She Cannot Hear the Sound of Her Own Weeping	55
Why Does the Bee Fly into the Little Iron Pagoda in the Garden?	56
Listening to John Ashbery	57
Fire in the Green Field	58
Upon Hearing a Child is Told the Prayers of Clasped Hands are not Heard	59
Rich Facts	60
Downpour	61
Days When I Can	62
She Is	63
Afterward	64
Torre De Pájaros	65
It Was Never a Question of Ladders	66
The Rain Carries on Its Back the Grief of Horses	69
Introit	70
Notes	71
About the author	73

Acknowledgments

Grateful acknowledgment is made to the editors of the following journals in which these poems, some in earlier versions, first appeared:

Cumberland Poetry Review: "Why She Cannot Hear the Sound of Her Own Weeping"

The Georgia Review: "Downpour"

Image: "I Was Lying in the Yard of the Methodist Church," "Nocturne: Swift Water Point," and "Of Musick"

The Journal: "After Looking at Bruegel," "Book of Names," "Cantata," "Reconsidering the Rift," "Sotto Voce" and "The White Slip"

The Kenyon Review: "Grace Notes" and "The Swing"

Mudfish: "Bronze Woman"

The Pennsylvania Review: "Botany"

Poetry: "Afterward" and "You Shall Be Weeping and Crying"

Seneca Review: "She Is" and "The Third Heaven"

West Branch: "Out of My Husband's Pockets"

In addition, some of these poems were first published in a chapbook, *There and Back*, by State Street Press, 1993. Among these, "Mary's Poem" was reprinted in *Divine Inspiration: The Life of Jesus in World Poetry*, Atwan, R., Dardess, G., and Rosenthal, P., eds. N.Y., Oxford University Press, 1998.

The author would like to thank the New York Foundation for the Arts, the Alumnae Association of Mount Holyoke College, the Constance Saltonstall Foundation for the Arts, and the Arts & Cultural Council for Greater Rochester for fellowships which made possible the writing of many of these poems.

I would like to express my deepest gratitude to Judith Kitchen for her generous and gracious reading of these poems. Special thanks also to Linda Allardt and Stan Rubin, long time mentors and friends. To those dear friends who have shared their work with me and read many of these poems, thank you. Finally, the writing of this book has been blessed by the love and patience of my husband Gerry.

Notations on the Visible World

One

Grace Notes

Smell of ash in the air, a distant burning,
and the clatter of wild turkeys,
the racket of sex;
the woods are full of it,
                              wing-
tipped, cry of the flicker
like some derangement of the senses, the steering
of fernlip towards the light, what little
we have.
              A low rolling
of thunder and the rain when it comes   falls
like a form of angelic restlessness,
an imagined sighing —
a bitter tonic after a long illness.

Violets bloom at the edge of the lawn
like the purple release of blood
under the skin.
                  Kyrie, says the flicker,
all desire and beginning. I doubt it.
This understory of gauzy brush not yet shaken out
is a shimmering scarcely achieved.
                                    The self
wants to sing,
for who can bear the containment of the trees,
the eyes' aptitude for green now?

The woods are full of it,
rain falling like a part of speech
nearly forgotten,
                    like grace notes from a page of music

held in the mind until now.

You Have Been Exiled Here for a Reason

The flawless performance of the finch
is evidence enough. Gold-drenched, it dips
under blue-bladed hosta, the parabola
of bleeding heart, jewel-
tipped,
       flickers, lifts into honeysuckle and ash
allegrissimo, glissando, but never

sotto voce,
       on which depend all the unnumbered things of the world:
dust and air, the scent trails of moths mapping the linked
corridors of dusk, the first-light prayers
of the nearly unredeemable.
                          Sotto voce's
what you hear as the grasses of the field
genuflect in the wake of your passing when you're no one,
the feet of the gravel clicking.

       Sotto voce, teach me to be a scholar of understatement,
to see on jewelweed's underleaf the snail's
script, to hear in the mountain's applause under rain
the revival of lacewing and shrew.
                          Sotto voce's
a kind of humming the body knows: back alleys
of nerve endings fuzz and sputter; something's lost
like a feather on a spiral drift
to an unmarked clutter.
                     It's where the trees
harness the darkness to do their work, *sotto voce*,
and the death-watch beetle in the oak, and the blackberry's sheen
dissolving like a host on the tongue.

                          Somewhere
a bell savors your distinction.
Sotto voce, one perfect pitch
in the absence of your ringing.

The White Slip

That you cannot take it off is true.
No surprise you are dancing in my white slip in the dream I have,
    acetate swirls in a night of ash.

Take off your white slip, my mother said, slip
of a willow, slip of a girl, green.

In my mother's house I ironed the white slip
they buried you in.
                    No surprise
things can't pass from the living to the dead: teapots and rings,
loaves of bread, the white slip of my letter
you never read.

Take off your white slip,
slip of a willow, of a girl, green.
If the willow loves water, we will need a river.

The white slip is a circle of ox-eye daisies
in the field I will lie down in —
                          There, where you are,
nothing is the dust that everything is: willow
and ash, water, this air and the light you loved,
the girl slipping away now
and forever

Some Nights

My brother wanders through my house lighting
gas burners again, setting matches to our mother's kitchen drawers.
Tonight as we sleep,
                      he descends the cellar stairs
and dismantles our father's furnace.
                                        Sometimes my brother's
looking for his twin, our dead sister. He tells me
how he saw her on TV or downtown:
                                  She was an angel.

      Yes, I tried to tell him, *I've never known that kind of love,*
paired before birth, your transparent
                  fingers touching —

          Some nights my brother appears
in his blue gauze shirt, stirring pots of rice over the stove,
a bird man starving. After supper
he throws the *I Ching* on the kitchen table a hundred times,
the *Book of Changes* our mother hides.

                  These summer nights
he's a boy again: in the stairwell of the apple tree
          my brother stretches
our father's army blanket across two limbs
and falls to earth —
                  He falls

through the stars' cold fingers, past nets of fishes
stamped with fiery gills, down
through the bottomless lake.

There and Back

It is your constancy I love,
how you are always there at the end of the road
whatever brings me out,
how the two of you never approach.

Strange to find such solace
in your presence on a summer night,
grazing like shadows over invisibly green pastures,
like part of a dream, your very thoughts.

In winter you stand motionless
as terra cotta in a blank white field,
recalling the Chinese emperor's horses
at the edge of another world, ready to depart,
saddles of snow on your smooth chestnut backs.

Content to roam this field,
what do you know of grief or human weeping,
creatures who could carry a man or woman on your backs
across the earth, whom I've never seen leap
for joy, nor in your dark stalls sleeping.

Out of My Husband's Pockets

— Isaiah 55: 12

Out of my husband's pockets I shake
       wood dust like rain, curled shavings, splinters and
       chips, the fortieth summer released
       from the hundred year pine;

In my husband's pockets I find
       trees, honey-fleshed oak, luminous whorls of birds-eye maple
              and butternut
       mimicking in darkness the slow beating of wings,
       the stern purity of ash, transparency of birch, the cool
       tempered fragrance of cedar and pine;

From my husband's pockets fall
       houses, rafters and beams, sawn two by fours, windowsills,
       walls, tedium of hammers, insatiable cry of the circular saw,
       the ten inch span of his spread fingers, the eight foot
       reach of his raised arm;

Out of his pockets fly
       the trimmed edges of doors continually closing
       on argument and embrace, shoe-molding kicked by a child,
       cupboards soiled by fingers reaching and lifting, the sill
       worn smooth by the elbows of the body leaning
       into the green press of leaves always singing at dusk
       the names of your children;

In the corners of my husband's pockets gather
       roots ground into salves, infusions of sassafras and willow,
       broad leaf of the linden shading the noon-hot house, furrows
       of bark for laying on the soul, resin and sap, sap and resin
       sticking to this world out of the whorled knot;

Out of my husband's pockets flow
        a continent of forests, cold lakes, wings of the blue jay
                bursting
        from the shattered limb, the red vole and pine martin,
        islands of pine leaning downriver, canyons without trees;
        and still they are clapping, the trees, the hills
        are singing and clapping,

Falling as dust out of my husband's pocket,
        falling like resinous tears, like tiny cymbals whispering,
        laughing and grieving, filling the air with the sweet
        scent of their torn flesh;

In the dim light of the basement float down
        these which have lain against the sweat of his chest;
        against the four chambers of his heart they have lain all day,
        and the muscles lifting and pulling, drawing in, drawing out

What has fallen from your house into his pocket
        onto the whorled grain of my fingertips,
        dust and sweat, the trees clapping, hills singing, the laying
        of hands on the living wood, cry of his labor,
        his error and love, the four chambers of his heart,

And what I fail to gather,
        wood dust like rain on the floor of my house.

A Reply

— Girl Reading a Letter, Vermeer

If for a moment you believe the heart
hangs on a word,
like the soul on a matter of faith —
that memory or desire might flare
like the red flame of the window drape flung back
into the dark corner, or that this light
surely must have passed through high branches,
layers of new leaves all morning long,

Observe how this outer light
articulates the smooth, high brow
and washes a blinding white the window ledge,
the curled half of the page
she's already read.   Oh, it hardly matters
that we'll never know who he is,
or her reply, for the story is always
the same: what's been said and left unsaid,
how the light changes.

I Was Lying in the Yard
of the Methodist Church

Looking into the skybox I made with my hands, the edges
of my fingers shutting out four odd wisps of clouds
and three vultures rising on the hot air of the parking lot.
I wanted to see the other side of that blue seamlessness
to the night numbers falling swiftly as clocks through the universe;
I wanted to look forward and backward with a kind of
nostalgia no god would understand, ghost thoughts
on the perimeter of that earthly grass. I wanted to rise up,
I was hanging by a thread like the cankerworm
I saw under the maple in my yard, its lovely green body
slipping down from danger on a nearly invisible rope.
In the yard of the Methodist Church the sky spread above me
like a wordless tract, except for the wheeling of three vultures
on the verge of some terminal bliss, slow and purposeful
as architects circling an original idea I couldn't grasp.
I wanted to apologize to the fringed black wings
vaporized into evening light above my blundering body in the grass,
to the cankerworm scaling the walls of air in my yard,
a swung bell pitched outside of human hearing
into the doxologies of the leaves I'd never enter:
I saw how plain I was in the yard of the Methodist Church.

Triptych

*1. Watching Firelflies in Rain
   at the Stroke of Midnight in My Back Yard*

To the east lightning opens the sky:
Lift up your hands to my copper rivers!
Neither here nor there, fireflies rise
and fall undisturbed by the rain, cool lanterns
keeping their appointments with the dark.
The woods circle the house like a curtain
that refuses to be drawn.
We have gone miles beyond indigo.
Gutter, deckboard, leaf, apostrophe, sigh,
small things, vast accompaniment,
the voice of an old god humming.

*2. Waking After a Sleepless Night,
   I Sit on My Deck Drinking Coffee*

The pink and white faces of the impatiens cannot shine,
like silver washed of its mineral sheen.
I listen to rain that will not stop, steady
as a procession of monks in green robes,
my husband's workboots crunching the gravel.
The fireflies gone now, hung
on the undersides of bushes, dripping,
like stones gone cold. *If everything
must be taken away. If.*   Rain
moistens my stiff-necked prayers,
small erosions.

3. *A Woman Assumes the Logic of Sleep*

> *Then one of the seraphs flew to me, holding a live coal that had been taken from the altar with a pair of tongs. The seraph touched my mouth with it.*
> — Isaiah 6:1-8

Everywhere the evidence of sparrows, the child's
sword plucked from the robin's nest, the seraph's tongs —
Who has seen the prophet's seared lips, dust and ash rising
holy, holy out of the woods steaming after rain?
Who has heard the song of the yellow-striped beetle, song of
the egg-ridden leaf, cleft in the rock cradling half a moth's wing,
isolate, near transparency of glass, everywhere
purses of darkness under moss, beetle slayers, annelid rings,
the pockets of light between oak and ash, song of bone
and hammer, of chisel and knife, inflection of a murderer's
half-sigh until out of the woods that old voice, ancient
as a tubercular scar, *Who will go, Who will I send?*
from this place, limb-wracked, light-struck.
The listing of names is not enough. Now at the edges,
wood satyr, yellow sulphur, a dense fluttering of spare
economies floats by, breviary for a life.

Botany

In the center of the large white flower
observe the bearded face,
how the two lowest stamens are purple feelers,
the yellow anthers like clever hands.

On nights such as these
the luminous petals seem to hover by themselves.
See how the moth flies to the dark center —
it leaves a scattering of gold dust:
we are not who we appear to be.

Each day I watch the blossoms close,
then open skyward, as if aspiring to something.
By night, the moth mullein, named
for beast and flower, practices its cool white deceit
by which its stationary blooms in darkness
endlessly repeat.

Judy,

You probably didn't know I was listening on the kitchen stairs.
    I couldn't see you cutting that hoodlum's hair
to the reptilian creak of his black leather jacket.
        I was afraid

of what he'd do to you. I wanted to save you
    the way you swept me up in your arms and carried me
downstairs the day I fell through the glass door in the attic.
        Sister who said I prayed

too loud in church as if our voices
    should be small on this earth. Twenty-six years later
I'm still not sure what killed you, not the driver who knocked you
        off your new bike that night you took a spin

around the block, not sex, not even those needles.
    I never told you about the Fourth of July we younger kids
pushed each other up and down the street
        in the shopping cart

you'd dragged home that summer. Past midnight
    we swerved onto the Avenue, wheelied back and forth
across the lanes until a car passed. Scared,
        we ditched the cart

and ran. *It was Randy and his gang,* Jimmy Adams said.
    I saw those hoods whipping their chains,
they were gold. Jesus, I shivered
        in the warm night air, loving it.

Nocturne: Swift Water Point

Under the starblack and smooth light
the river whispers your names, *you you you*

hushed as the voices of women on the porch below,
names rising like the secret of mayfly and fish, like the silk

of blue heron slipping past the linden outside. Night freighters
glide past on the river, strung with lights. Speckle of moon

on my face, on my sister's white nightgown still whirling
in the room where nails stick down through roofboard and beam

like Jesus' cross. My grandmother breathes deep and low
in her bed, hair like a white halo, and I'm praying for rain

on the roof to shut out this dream where I'm drowning —
He calls me away to that place where the river speaks to me

with its mouths of moss, its lichen tongues iron scented,
bells of red columbine laughing, our bodies curled on dry needles

until the rain falls like my grandmother's words
Before you were born — I try to imagine not breathing, darkness

and nobody there as she peels peaches at the table, fingers
deft as fish in water, orange fish slipping into the blue-flecked bowl,

but where are my brother and sisters? There are so many gaps
and our wooden raft still twirls downstream on a blazing

sheet of light where I left them swimming circles
in an old tin pail, bellies of turquoise and gold that go round

and round in my love's arms, in my grandmother's hands
dripping with the fluency of tears, in the swallows'

sweep and glide from the linden's stained leaves that say
night now; say *sing again*, ships that go down to the sea, rain

that touches the river's lips. Say *mayfly, fish, blue heron*,
say *love*, this breath that goes in, breath that goes out

Walking on Water

The boat drinks the cool length of the river slowly
as fish race past to their caves of sleep,
recess of rock and weed. We float up with the evening
to the first stars: Orion sleeps low
in the eastern sky, his club raised in a futile
gesture against the night. O violet, O indigo,

We have all dreamed of walking on water,
wished for the knowledge of its soft footings.
The channel light blinks green, green.
How to assume such lightness and not look back?
Now the pale moon rises like a balloon let go
when we weren't looking, like the sister who will not come home,
all night her soft shoes dancing on the river.

Translation

Largely a day of diminutives,
                               tap and flicker of chitin
lips on moss, legs hot as wires negotiating
grass columns minute

and particular, white cabbage butterflies in the field,
a trembling morse code, there
                               not there.
Close your eyes
and the day's a stutterer's paradise —
    Begin Begin Begin   say the moistened bodies of crickets
in a streambed of sound that might be pure memory
                               but for the *hush* and *now*
of wind come from uncanny distances to move leaves
soaked with night-rain and two days' sun.

It's hard to see
             what history's
being shaped here: the coneflower drops a neon petal   or two,
      now the *plunk* of a hard green globe
the linden tree's been working on and let go without so much
as a tremor and sigh.

Desiring the Solicitude of Rain

1

So what is it you're looking for now
in the ceremony of leaves?
The day gives in to a snapping of white shades, the wind's
a fist of nothingness, the dayglow orange lilies in your garden
an unlikely delight.

The hot wind refuses to bring rain
as predicted, the way a life refuses to reveal itself
until much later, in sleep, perhaps,
when you see your whole life

collapsed to a point
like a small object carried off in a suitcase
on a trip that meant nothing to you then, swinging high
and low, high and low,
                    the field of weeds unbroken before you.

2

And then it's clearly there, or almost,
an otherwordly nearness, the sky about to open
and speak, the umbel leaves dropping with their virtual loss,
blackened but spectral.
                    In a moment
it will all be roil and spume, clatter
and cymbal clash, the simple eye changed as in the click of a shutter
announcing *then* and *now*,

the hands held open to the air's coinage,
palm upward,
the bone dry skin waiting.

3

On this trip you will be allowed to take
nothing, neither object nor love,
not the one you bent over in sleep tonight to touch
but did not touch for fear of waking further,
eyes open, looking up at what could only be a dream and you left.

When at last the rain comes
it comes like the mouth of a god in total darkness singing,
Oh you did not know your grief was salt, your body an ocean —

so rich and deep a resonance, it wakes even the trees
you walk between without pockets to carry change or photographs,
here where you cannot see the falling

of hands, fingers and bones falling, petiole
and crushed leaf, sweet earlobe, gnat wings and moth filament,
lash and lip falling like rain through hands
to the untroubled earth.

Of Musick

The phrase must be held in the imagination.

> — James Bobb, to the Lutheran Church of
> the Incarnate Word Choir on a motet by
> Antonio Lotti (1667-1748).

Otherwise you will arrive too quickly.
Hold back, lean like the singer
gently into the summer evening, the black dome
of the maple where an anonymous bird begins
something more sorrowful than your heart can hold,
and you rise above the night insect's tight harmonies
toward what you cannot see, but feel the shape of
distending the darkness, until something answers,
one note riding the other, that moment
of dissonance like the friction of two bodies
before the letting go —

Why not linger before the sweet wrenching away
from the note which is mortal, too, and the bird,
and the dispassionate night reading over and over
that keening and shurring, for that is how you see it,
no less real than the moon's obligatory light
now pressing its assembly of skulls
on the rooftops and trees.

Now that you're almost there, it releases
a final trill and flourish, like the irrepeatable inventions
of that early unknown singer, a last gesture reaching out
to hold the night and every thing that trembles in it, that singer,
this voice lost between breath and sigh, so that you almost see it:
a notation on the visible world fading to near silence
and you wonder how long you have stood here
listening to shadows ornamenting shadows
in the tender good night.

Two

"You Shall Be Weeping and Crying"

— Cantata #103, J. S. Bach

When the new director of the church choir tells me
You're really a soprano, I pretend not to hear,
an alto at heart, though I'm shaken by the way my voice
can fill that lofty room with high notes thrown out
like a rope from an unsteady boat.

I'd rather be earth and burnt grass continuously
rumbling beneath the soprano's silver arcs of light
astonishing everyone who looks at the sky,
recognized by those with their feet on the ground
who know where truth and beauty really lie.
I'll settle for being the nearly anonymous leaves
of the yellow trumpet vine at the corner of my house
clarifying the final gesture of that ascending line.
Yes, only the altos can make a desert of C's bloom
in a room of waning afternoon light, make scarcity
seem like someone's knocked at your door with a gift.

I could extend my vocal range with faithful
practicing of ever higher scales, though it's hard for me
to stray far from home, close to what I love.
Secretly, it's the melody I love to sing when I'm alone.
In the shower, wrapped in clouds of steam, I become
vaporous and obscure, gone to heaven and belting out
Amazing Grace as if I know how wide God's mercy really is,
drawing those bars to a bluesy close so I can begin
the Handel aria I've always longed to sing.

When I open the curtains to see myself in the slowly
clearing mirror, I struggle to find my part
in the Bach Cantata we're doing, intervals of suffering
offered like a trial to the singer, notes that only make sense
when they're sung with the others, like rungs on a twisting
ladder that suddenly fit into place and I can almost
tell who I am, where I am going —

Still, it's not easy, all those voices, all that breath
raised in a single cry that seems outside of human hearing,
Ihr werdet weinen und heulen.

When They Heard the Lord Calling

— Genesis 3: 9

Where are you?

        the late morning breeze
parting the grasses behind them, a mild disturbance

in the upper reaches of the plane tree,
the earthbound pulse and hum of every living thing bowing
before the sound of footsteps pushing aside and snapping

the canebreak at the edge of the woods
where they liked to stand before darkness fell
        on the cooling meadow,
the man's finger pressing a just-picked berry

to the woman's lips, they could not bear
to be loved so, and all the small creatures of the field chirring
because, because —
small lies and a bitter exit?

        For all we know
it had the sweetness of the veery's song, clear, bell-like,
a little sadness in it without the breathiness of anything human.

Remnants and Sudden Clarities

The late afternoon light
shifts in the garden, green of minute shadows
        rippling.

Purple blooms of spiderwort bell out of the shade
an inexhaustable silence.
Fern leaflets shiver like touched skin.

        All day slow arrivals, drift of
cottonwood seed down under the damp succulence
of the coneflower's lowest leaf. The white petals of Siberian iris float
as if on water and not on this air that a beetle scales,
rigged to a blade of grass.
                                    At the edge of the woods
the hosta billows, blue leaves a child crawled under
        (stones and clothespin doll,
beadstrings, a beetle shell) —

So much progeny and the scent of something
I'll never name, contagion
        of sweetness.

Angel of the Annunciation

> Detail of the *Lehman Annunciation,* Botticelli

Even Botticelli knew that no lithe
limbed creature could carry a message of such weight,
though the stalk of lilies denies it and the wings
unfurled like wisps of smoke, the drapery
roiled by a sudden turbulence we'll never feel.

Head bent, this round-thighed angel
seems overcome by what he's about to say.
It doesn't matter that she isn't on this page,
for we'll soon see how difficult it is
to bear such news to its completion.
We know where the nine gold rays of light fall
here in this world where everything is rational,
the neatly receding salmon-colored panels of the marble floor,
the gray pilasters vanishing into shadow
as if it's all a matter of perspective
that can't be argued with.

She must have known there was no way out
when she saw those white sails light at the door of her room
and thought how she should have gone to the market
to buy pressed olives, or visited her cousin
in the village just over the hill, knowing how quickly
the lilies would drop their trumpet blooms on the cold floor,
and the strange burst of wind, exciting
for a moment, settle to a near perfect stillness
she'd come to live with.

Later it's a surprise to find out
just how humbly she bows her plain head, eyes
closed, a marvel of acquiescence; behind her
a crimson coverlet flames out of the unlit bedroom, dark
as the womb, its velvet curtains drawn back.

Mary's Poem

When she heard infinity
whispered in her ear, did the flashing
scissors in her fingers fall
to the wooden floor and the spool unravel,
the spider's sly cradle
tremble with love? Imagine

how the dry fields leaned
toward the news and she heard, for a moment,
the households of crickets —
When she answered, all things shifted, the moon
in its river of milk.

And when she wanted to pluck
her heart from her breast, did she remember
a commotion of wings, or the stirring
of dust?

Nativity

> — Piero della Francesca, 1475

They say you painted this one late in life
and so it seems, all things turned
to shadows of themselves,
this ghost of a cow and the shepherd
who raises his arm, a thin banner waving.

And yet, an extraordinary light
falls evenly as night on this countryside.
Far off, a stream winds like a strip of shiny satin.
From my window, the neighbor's low roof
is a field of snow. Perhaps
it's so in Arezzo, I've read of the particular clarity
of the sunlight on the rocky ground,

across the smooth, tilted face
of this girl, her infant son reaching up from a corner of her robe,
a sea of folds on dry ground.
But this is a celebration! Five barefoot angels
sing or strum their mandolins.
The unearthly cow
lifts her head and bellows.
Hungry and tired, old Joseph
looks without amazement at the singing cow.
Behind him the distant city, each blue window painted in,
is already there, each life lived out
more or less in suffering.

It is midday, not night,
but the cattle low as they should
and the angels are singing their hearts out.
Outside, toward evening now, snow falls
as a black bird waits on the roof of the shed
ready to pluck each note rising
from strings we cannot see.

Meditation

We're lucky to live in a woods, I say
as we sit on our porch enjoying the summer evening.

If only we had a river, you say,
as we drink our cool lemonade.

I think of our small son,
how every night he tries to step
into the train nosing the edge of the page
or pluck the pictures from his storybooks:
willingly, I lift the lighted candle to his stormy lips,
or make the bluebird on a paper bough
sing in the palm of my hand.

Look, I say, *the river's all in your mind anyway.
Be a Buddhist. Give it up.*

Soon our son will climb aboard a train
that will carry him into other woods
with rivers and boughs full of birds
he can and cannot touch.

Everything is fire.
And about questions of rivers and loss
I have little to say.

We're lucky to live in a woods.

Book of Names

> *The wooden bed of the clock comes from the stout*
> *railings which John had erected in his youth at the*
> *side of Haw Bridge to prevent drunkards from falling*
> *into the Severn as they left the pub.*
>
> — B. E. Pegler, *A Historical Guide to the Parish*
> *Church of Tirley Gloucestershire*

Not enough that God knows but the whole world
knows, the worn fingertips passing over the page of names
lightly as over a forehead in sleep,
beside each one his or her occupation
or lack: he was a beggar, she bore
an illegitimate child.

Wasn't it enough that the sparrows
in the hedgerows turned their faces in passing,
tired of his mild ranting, the spastic arm
relentlessly carving the air, or that each time
her womb released the weight of itself she remembered
the sound of stones stinging the windows, the days
she slipped through the churchyard alone,
the thin fabric of the choir's voices?

And now their lives come to this
before a stranger's eyes,
compressed into the tight flares and flanges and dots
of ink, the few flourishes given
a life of milk and dirt. Above the traveller
who signs another book, the tower clock tolls,
its works made of everything that touched or turned this soil,

winnowing machine and chaff cutter, bicycle pedal, roasting jack
and bean drill, beer barrel and farmyard weights
lovingly assembled by the village carpenter

to call the people to come and praise their Maker,
the one act of tenderness in a story
where the child was flower and ruination,
and the tin cup banging the empty air
was the best that you could do.

After Looking at Bruegel

Why does God dream? Why do angels carry swords?
— Tristan, age three and a half

You point to Christ's pale face lost in a swarm
of topsy-turvy villagers and tell me these pictures are the dreams
       of God.
I could tell you in this world wings are not enough, the angels
are warding off with their swords whatever will wake
these dreams into being, as snow falls outside into the same
crepuscular gloom the hunters and their dogs return from.
His sleep is a hunger we feed, and here we are, ships
tossed on a tourmaline sea, your favorite scene,
magpie on the gallows, skaters
on the perilous ice.

Reconsidering the Rift

I am thinking about error and beauty
and how it all began, the exactitude of spotted lungwort
and the meticulous divisions of the painted fern;

I am thinking about antimony and grace
and what constitutes an act of God, how the eagle's
7,000 feathers weigh a mere pound and a half in the human hand;

I am telling our son which is the meat-eater,
which is the plant-eater, not how all things devour one another
in the end, necessitating the red worm and dung beetle,

as I study his picture of the red-tailed hawk,
wings striped and speckled with green, gold, and blue bursting
into one crimson flame, its head thoughtfully turned

as if considering the spectacular descent.
I am thinking about the richness of our hurt as the veery in the pine
repeats a sweet descending sigh in the face of evening;

I watch the two-faced leaves of the linden and sassafras
go dark to light, dark to light, weighing
the possibility of transubstantiation, how one thing could be
        another ...

He is telling me it is the hawk who is beautiful, and I see how it is,
how *not to worry*, the small footed creature at the bottom of the page
always slips away because it is *too fast,*

grace in the mouth of a child like the lamb wrapped
in the python's absent arms he is sure will rise up to walk again.
I am thinking about error and beauty and how it all began.

Trying My Lines Aloud on the Back Porch

Foolish enough, I look up from reading aloud
to see the face of a deer gazing at me, listening,
a wad of leaves fringing the long curve of her mouth.
How she's come to hear me above the squirrels' chittering
and the August swell of the field I don't know.

I am glad my words do not frighten her away.
Perhaps the music is too easy, tricking her into believing
words have no power, and the way the tawny line
of her shoulder relaxes only proves my lack of toughness.
Perhaps I do not speak enough of the world's difficulty

to chase her away; it's probably my dark
brown eyes she's reading, as I am hers, and now the bits
of crisp white apple I can hear her chewing are not
my words she's tasting. She's tasting the end of summer.
It's true I am not speaking the right language,

but I'm willing to enter those woods to study
the leaves' texts, the way her body slips soundlessly
in and out of the leaves, as if what's best is what's left
unspoken. I'm glad the deer can fill her belly here.
I know it's only the plunder in my yard she's after,

though I hope my lines about cool water
rising from the stream's dry stones in those woods
offer some respite from the heat of this day,
an invitation to return with the others to sleep
all night under the trees in my yard.

The Wild Boy Retreats to His Father's Truck

The wild boy dances on the roof of his father's truck.
Tonight the river laps quietly as if content with a life
flowing one way. Things can change though, wind,
the paradise of a storm. He bangs and stutters, monkey limbs
climbing the air. She loves the first calm before sleep
when she can hold him. *Let him go*, the father says.

She thinks of the way the river goes: what's silver now
is always something else, the current's black tempers,
the scarlet bloom of gills opening and closing.
The wild boy's voice is like a ball thrown into the air
he might or might not catch. A wail, or a song.
Swarms of gnats congregate on the bank, their invisible centers
shifting. *Worlds within worlds*, she thinks.

From the house, wind chimes. Far-off, the bassoon
      of a freighter's horn.
He draws pictures crouched on the roof of his father's truck:
planes, bombs, walls of fire falling on little men.
His pen waves in the air. Soon papers will be flying.
She wants to love this state of grace. The river goes on
and the wild boy cries because it's never right,
the near paradise of storms.

After a Time of Trouble

I would welcome your company tonight
walking in the wooded valley below the houses,

on the deer path worn down between trees
wound with vines already curling into flame.

At any moment we could turn back toward
the lights of the houses coming on now.

I would welcome your company, here,
under the great linden in my yard, leaves riddled

with disease and still moving over us singing
something about a *Jesus for a broken river,*

coolness that we could bathe our feet in
as we watch the lit undersides of the leaves

waving like prayer flags someone lifted up all day,
and the little Buddhas on the stone path.

Tonight we could talk about the words
we found today, *what your neighbor said,*

the word I found in my son's red dictionary,
alembic, as if lifted clean out of a pocket of fire:

anything that transforms, purifies, or refines.

I'd welcome your company even as we part
and I stand to watch you wave, your body

turning into darkness, not a word needed, no
nod of the head, small gesture of consolation.

"The Third Heaven"

What if it is the sound of voices
under the glasses turned upside-down on the pantry shelf
       (whisperings, small declarations, articles of faith sung
              on a single pitch),
or the bell no one else hears ringing out of a sky terraced with clouds
the color of ripe melons spilling their seeds into the evening
that keep her alive? And the way she holds her ear
to the magenta blooms of the sweet pea — arterial,
       flushed, gone blue in a day,
as if this might be the source of a new invention, the abundance
of lost things speaking everywhere.
Why not let her gaze at the nails burning the wood deck —
       iron oxide, meristem, cambium, fixatives, ores,
              a woods in bloom —
the dilemma of seeing too much in a world
that requires her confinement. It would have to be
a terrible prayer asking for love, the forgetting of whiskey
on the brain. She knows the way the sky turns
the color of those flowers, night coming down,
is more than a narrowing of the day to pure longing
for a far away place: Machu Picchu,
       green walls, five kinds of corn buried, so many secrets!
Don't tell. This could be the beginning of her salvation. Don't say
you heard her singing *green walls, green walls*
to the tune of the wind justifying its terrible deeds.

Bronze Woman

She is pure attention; she cannot be swerved
by my hand waving downriver, the diffident glide of our canoe.
Seated above the granite shore, she leans toward the object
    of her longing,

bare shoulders pressed forward, her naked back
a ripely drawn bow, smooth and polished as this blue-green
water, the cold depths we trail in.

And who could not love her? How carefully
she has arranged herself behind the bank of apricot lilies
shielding her small breasts, the indigo hollow

of her throat rising to the pointed chin, *someone's* chin,
and the boyish, closely cropped hair even the wind
cannot move now.

Rounding the island, we are caught in her gaze,
outward but indrawn to a length of shadow, knowledge
    she will not impart.
These are her only declarations: the high note of a cricket

stammering under the once liquid fires of her verdigris foot,
at dusk, the copper bellies of the swallows upbraiding
the lilies, vying for her tenderness.

Granite Trail

— for my mother

Islanded, from the overlook, stone outcropping,
we step down with dusklight into the granite rift
intimate as memory (we have been here before):
tree-layered, leaves poised absolutely,
blue-green, silvered; near stillness speech laden,
unbroken, briefly a peace between us. We drop
down to the hard place, cushionless bottom, no fern,
no moss, to the end of cataclysm, time: rocks
toppled, each harboring a small cave of darkness.
What darkness will do to this place keeps us moving.
The light from across the river stipples
the columns of the trees, wreck of luminescence.
We climb out of mothlight, the upper woods
shot with bird cry, eerie, but here nothing, the hour
floating upon itself, no history between us.
We climb hard, steadily up to rock's
smooth carapace, each step a motive for love.

August Latitudes

In the limbs of the dying linden
all morning the spider's taut filaments
flash like strings of a harp wildly dispersed,
intermittent signals of light
caught at the edge of whatever
this world is.

                        Beneath the linden,
stalks of late blooming lobelia burn
ice blue, little flames licking the shadow air.
A purple ground beetle scurries
from the steel tongue of my trowel as if
from a meeting with the devil;
the Chinese forget-me-not
bursts into a scattering of seed
voluminous as night.

Why am I afraid to do the soul's work?

Open, click, lock
       and release, something says, or I think it does,
and the low rasp of a frog in its dank understudy,
curlicue of birdsong
latching the ear like a sweet hook.

What do I know but words?
What the wind brings, we try to name:
the armature of beetles, rust, the mechanics of
sorrow, and not the thing itself —

                        It's a small thing, door-
hinge, leaf-hinge, something invisible
turns on the air.

The day's a sum of light.
How this beauty's a lush impediment to sight! On furrowed bark,
the pupal husk of a cicada, split,
emblem of pure emptiness I'd climb into
but cannot

where I've no business, in this flesh,
blue flames of lobelia ticking, taut strings
lashing, little death maps, a calculus of sudden and slow,
curved space marked down to
nothingness
                but for this, my weak mathematics:

I build on a premise of joy.
Not knowing is the central act.
In leaf light bearing down late summer.

Banishment of the Alleluia

Who could listen to the continuous sound of God's weeping
in the names of the flowers and all their little
deaths, dropwort and tansy,
fleabane and vetch;
                and who could listen to his repeated supplications
in the absence of the oriole's voice, its old ribbon of notes
perplexing the air outside the kitchen window
where surely he must see the broken
dish on the linoleum floor and the unspoken words
turning back on the heart like the body's own nails —

                                            Listen
to his endless petitions in the matchstick
held to the wind, salvation's notices snuffed out
again and again —

Even the sound of the rose petals' ticking in the blaze of high noon
is the sound of his own weeping
in the face of the crazy man who calls himself the bones of dogs;

can't you hear his weeping
                                      in the shoe's emptiness,
in the slow breathing of the child with shoulder blades
like the nubs of wings which were never ours
until his tongue is thick with it

and iron and lead have no weight in the air
that holds everything his before it falls away
and the little two step
                            dance in the dust begins,

one note, two notes,

small bells ringing in the mouth of the wind

The Voice Outside

is September rain falling on the house
of the child waiting for someone to come,

but now it is you and the lights coming on
along the street where crickets have been singing

all evening, inaudible now under rain,
the way it is easy to forget what was said.

The living work of the rain is all we know now
and it is good, even the form of sadness it conjures,

silver road washed with water and light and
darkness beginning, road of all the right steps,

all the wrong ones in rain you'd walk in
if not for the children in the next room you cannot leave,

not yet. So you sit in the living room under lamplight
and the weeping fig that the wind blows into shapes

across the page, shadow of the aleph, little ciphers,
serifs of an unknown script flickering,

Is it the petal that blooms out of the darkness?
Or darkness that blooms from the flower?

rain talking to itself and never lonely,
quieting now, and you hear a bird, or two,

never *a capella*, the rain, and the voices
of your children calling you home.

Three

The Swing

The far light on the lawn, this humming in the grass
swells out of the night the crickets first sing like the source

of midsummer before it begins with the hand
        on the small of the back
swinging the child on the fresh cut plank hung from the maple,
      swish-ticking

through green tunnels of air. Sweep and utter, sweep and utter
what's now: it's the mood, the hour, the light, the day, the night

the mother cannot hold back. Novitiates, the crickets are singing
the present is the past is the present, the sum of our perpetual erasure,

dust kicked up by the heel lightly brushing the ground.
The crickets' singing is the gold rain of winged seed, a little rough,

a little sweet, is what she hears, the mother swinging in the body
of the child riding the miles of the leaves, backward and forwards

in the swell of midsummer the moment before their faces
      are marked
by leaf and light and an inkling of love and the origin of time.

Cantata

So it is possible that the slenderest
of faiths depends on the last grace notes of the oriole at dusk
or the soprano singing the Bach aria
in the high windowed room, stunning God's drum
transposed to the only space we know.

The harmonies created by voices wrapping
round one another in the central fugue, curiously
repeated in the urgent twinings of the morning glory vine
about the vertical posts of the porch rail,
may be the only way we can feel the infinite texture of God's skin
passing over our fingers and lips.

Who wouldn't want to believe
that the slow and steady plucking of the cello
is really the beating of wings in no hurry to wake you
from the dream you're in,
surely a rehearsal of something better to come.

No need to wonder if these liquid
outpourings are nothing more than a way to forget
your other self, the skin lamps of Buchenwald
and the steamy excavations of jungles,
the way you wake up sweating in the middle of the night
unable to remember what you have done —

If your culpability is greater
than that of the screaming lion or cricket
mindlessly strumming, don't you deserve more?
And the white baton so gracefully waving in the conductor's hands
before the almost radiant faces of the singers,
what relation does it bear to the mud on the ape's paw
swinging through the shimmering grove?

Don't think about it.
At the next crescendo, when the hairs
on your neck rise, it's not just you, something's gone
twang in the universe:
high in the Andes, a bell rings.

Dark outside now, incense rising
like your own breath, the sure simplicity of the final
chorale, remarking on everything that has gone before,
assures you of a place in heaven
before silence falls on the great room slowly
emptying, on the goat on the mountain,
and nothing else.

Baptism Of Christ

— Piero della Francesca, c. 1442

It's a wonder Christ steps into that polished rivulet
(decorous, glazed, it could be glass;
a satin ribbon winding).

      Still, it's a view so generous
it deserves your absolute attention. Everywhere
a clear, unstinting light shapes all things
equally, the columns of Christ's legs repeating
the tree's bleached pillar, the carved folds of angel robes
and the figure of a nearly naked man
bending at the water's edge.

      He could be anyone.
And isn't it hopeful, this Christ
like a Tuscan farmer armed with a giant's ears
and wiry shocks of hair, reminding you
of the unkempt uncle you haven't seen in years?
And a sky translucent as your grandmother's
blue china cup you emptied and held
to the kitchen window?

      It's what's off-center
that surprises: that angel resting
a pale hand on its companion's shoulder
catches your eye with a look at once mildly
accusing and pitying, until you see yourself there,
afraid the light will shift too suddenly,
the look of one who keeps the world
at a distance —

         the deepest layers
of the tree's velvet crown, the wildflowers
sprigging the foreground, offering brief
refreshment from the hard word of this life,
the day's impending heat.

    Just when you think meditation
is revelation, you can't endure the stillness.
All along you've been longing to hear
the clapping of dove wings above
the plash of feet stepping into shallow water,
its nearly soundless trickle over
the shaggy brow, closed lid of the eye,
like that first cool hand parting
your feverish hair.

Agony in the Garden

> — Andrea Mantegna, 1460

And suppose they were all to awaken
at this very moment?
Hardly a garden to sleep in, anyway,
this mineral world, one nearly leafless tree.
And the log thrown across the silver blade of a brook
as if there were somewhere to escape to!
Not that they have any trouble
sleeping on the hard ground, mouths open,
jowls gone slack, each breath, each sigh's
a visible departure.
                        If Judas points the way
to soldiers in the middle ground
where something is always happening,
why do the rabbits linger on the open road
at such an hour, the sky tinged
with green light? Oblivious to angels,
they whisper so the others may sleep,
like creatures from a child's book
playing in a garden at dusk,
their voices softer than water rippling,
less than a stirring of leaves.

Why She Cannot Hear
the Sound of Her Own Weeping

Beneath the linden, he rubs his rough hands
on his jacket before he bends to break the heartwood open.
She stands at the window where she's heard before
the fury of his hammer, saw, and axe those days
when anger rises between them like a dark sap.

She thinks of the hushed invitations
of the leaves, the brief possibilities of love, his dead father
who hardly spoke to him, but named like children
the boxalder, shagbark hickory, the ironwood,
wild cherry and sassafras. Behind the glass,

She watches how his love holds the elements
together, iron, oak, and air, then saves what's left
to heat the house all winter. It's nothing
she ever says that brings him back, but something farther off,
she thinks, like the cry of a particular bird, woods-deep.

Why Does the Bee Fly into the Little Iron Pagoda in the Garden?

Perhaps the scent of wax drippings arouses desire.
In the garden nothing's by accident: these lilies bloom apricot,
those the color of a child's sun on white paper.
So many places for the bee to enter and why this moment

of shade in the garden? A prisoner once heard God's voice
in water rippling outside. His friend likened prayer
        to bees making honey.
The iron lantern rests on the rock like the idea of something holy.
Some people want to be seared with light and never forget.

Listening to John Ashbery

Tonight we have come to hear
the poet read in the museum,
his words a thick swell of water
drowning, releasing me, spill of moonlight
caught in amber glass and let go, leaping
ineluctable fish pursuing me as I listen
to the soft, constant jangle of his pockets,
ordinary silver, what the hands
have held all day, columns of pennies
stacked on bathroom shelves, in closets,
my father's dish of coins and keys
and paper slips atop the mahogany bureau
I never touched, like something holy,
the long steel shears in his small hands
trimming the hedge to perfection, green boundary
against air and all he could never say, pausing
to listen to the inhuman sweetness
of cardinal or robin, at his feet a fallen
bouquet of twigs and shiny leaves
to be gathered and swept away.

Fire in the Green Field

Snow everywhere and this stillness,
the way the mind shuts down, days that go on
like unanswered prayer, though what do we know
of our voices and the way they echo back?

Last night I stood at the storm door watching my sons
huddle in their homemade caves, waiting for news
of the enemy and fresh munitions in the hour of the long shadow.
The sky's slate pressed down on a sulfurous ledge
when the singing of peepers, *hyla crucifer*,

rose at the back of my brain, sweet admonition
from damp bark and leaf mold, a resurrection chorus
I knew had to be memory, the body stirring up
old music, green work against all odds
like those small encampments out there
in the cold, that burning.

Upon Hearing a Child Is Told the Prayers of Clasped Hands Are Not Heard

I'm praying in snow, the fierce objectiveness of snow
falling like the idea of the infinite,
I'm praying the voluptuousness of snow and minor wind,
the catechism of oak leaves shaking the answers
down. I want the prayer of expedience,
the prayer of good form and the beautiful hour,
of dew and raw light.

I'm praying with hands clenched,
hands at my sides, fingers in pockets, knuckles
on lids, palm to wet cheek. I'm praying the trembling
of snow on eyelids and quaking lips, for the laying
down of the body on snow, snow on the body,
for the hand still moving on the heart,
one time, one time.

I'm praying north pole to south,
mantle and core, I'm praying crystal
and flux, the prayer of condensed matter.
I'm praying like the devil, as my grandmother would say.
I'd pray without tongue or ear,
I'd work myself into the muteness of stone
if that's what You want.

Rich Facts

If you are weary, think of what sleeps for a year and more,
or twenty, the African lungfish sunk in the mudflats
of a drought-stricken river, wrapped in its hard cocoon.
Consider what travels far to become what it is:
tiny glass eels, salt-loving orphans born in the warm Sargasso Sea,
drift three years to the mouths of their freshwater rivers,
thickening and darkening, preparing for change.

If your accomplishment is great, your expectation lofty,
take note of the garden spiders in their one acre meadow
spinning enough silk in a week to circle the moon,
or the purple hairstreak always hovering in the trees' canopy —
Imagine if you hardly touched down
like the weak-legged swift, unable to stand,
eating and drinking on air.

If you are full of wisdom, ponder the bat's
uncanny interpretations of the dark, the firefly's and cecropia moth's;
or the astonishment of the road-flattened mole risen into the night
he thought he knew best. If you are impatient to finish
remember all that hesitates before it goes on:
the severed cry of the loon in your presence,
the one who stumbles in your path.

Downpour

I will go back to the day it rained in the late summer garden,
a merciless rain that plucked my deaf ears
open, such wild applause that had nothing to do with me,
nor the way I'd arranged the broad-leafed hostas
in a half-moon, the laddered spires of lobelia in between,
and then the lilies, loosestrife, and spiky monarda
for rain to fall on, which in the end made no discernible
difference, the whole woods clamoring, a ceaseless drumming
that said, *So much singing cannot be shut out:*
Rise and walk away, and for a moment it was all Mississippis,
cane-backed chairs and spinning reeds, the soft secrecies of
flesh spiralling underneath, but I tell you, it had the absolute
certainty of answered prayer. It was what it was —
rain — having no use for words like *redemption,*
redemption mimicking its course, undefiled by gutter
and downspout, rock and ripped leaf. It was a litany with purpose,
a near monotone that played and leapt to its conclusion
in spite of my foolishness, white flames dancing on a glassy tabletop.
Yes, I know it was simply the result of all the conditions
        that permitted it,
but my God, how it laughed at me, the rain and the green flesh
declaring itself alive.

Days When I Can

I'm thinking about the highway of the broom,
your broom and the rake you dragged across your lawn
that fall the leaves fell so late we raked
        until Christmas.
                      That morning
you woke up after New Year's, legs paralyzed
and barely forty, I was circling the green kitchen tiles
because it was something I could do;
        I wanted to go down
                      on my knees.
Instead of weeping, I swept. I saw
how lovely and instructive the movements of the broom,
and the hands held just so, one above the other,
        fingers wrapped
                lightly around
that slender instrument requiring the cheek's turning,
the merest looking down at how the feet lead
step/glide,   *step/glide* the stiff skirt
        of the broom lifting
                      the day's litter.
I celebrate those rare days I sink to the kitchen floor,
wet rag in hand to wash away what the broom's
left behind. Days when I can
        I think of you
                and how honorable
is the slight bending of straw,
praise for the body's give and take, but mostly
for the heart, the way your heart was,
        among the few
                cheerful — true —
and it wasn't easy, the pulling of the rake
to your tilted hip, slow
waltz for the seasons you'd been
        teaching us.

                In memory of D.C., 1958-1998

She Is

crouched down to see past bridgework
and creek's bend, mirrored silver, then blue:
under green overhangs a black so still
it seems fixed, at any hour
starless.

       Under the leaves' elaborations
see her: hunkered down, toe-hold in mud, hand
into water reaching the coolnesses of fishform and old light,
ochre updraft of leaf-litter, little destroyers: crayfish,
striped minnows havocked, surface strider
and sucking nymph, past

       glint of sedge and pale scum. Minutiae of iris imagined,
self dreaming of the self. The hand withdraws
dripping, nails ooze-riddled, in its palm, shining, star-
marked, the soft wet belly of something else
and half a life in darkness.

A rippling occurs
and the eye adjusts to its losses, faint
adumbrations of crumbled stone, maples, shadow of a house.

Afterward

The wind is all innuendo, stirring up the rain drenched leaves
        of the sugar maple.
Today I could say the wind is a green river flowing east,

calling me to swim its channels and leave my alluvial self.
I imagine rising where I can see my children on the lawn:

How beautiful they are, gliding like skaters
who could lift off at any moment! And there I am disappearing
        again

in the dip under my father's hedge where no one can find me,
my cheek against my cool stone globe, its dry continents.

Nights, the wind has entered our house and curled around
our bodies after love, leaving us desolate.

The wind will never lose itself on the thorns of my small rose bush.
Its silk rags are pure imagination.

Torre De Pájaros

They fell twenty years down from your book of Spanish poetry;
from the peonies in our mother's garden
they fell twenty years
down,
        these magenta petals —

        The hands
of my two-year-old son
                reached for their silk territories:
    the soft crush of
his fingers could have released
drifts of summer light,
        luz de verano;

or the sound of our high voices singing
beneath the linden trees the old hymns you taught us,
    notes rising up
             into the wafers of still green;

at his touch
their drained reservoirs could have filled with water again, *agua,*
    un milagro de agua, rain swollen streams
flowing across my kitchen floor —

I know this about you:
how carefully you placed them between the pages,
between these *canciones de pájaros y agua*;
how they would have delighted you,
the slow retinue of petals
falling like feathers from a tower of birds in another kingdom.
Still, you said nothing.

And I closed the book again.

It Was Never a Question of Ladders

1.

She slips into the room singing under your breath.
Repeat the calendar days like a prayer,
exactly what you know about the correspondence
between groundwater
                        and sky, the sure weight
of the cup you hold in your hands.

When she speaks of your body as a compass needle flickering
in the slow eye of the universe,
                        turn back
to your studious geography, the names of States recited
in alphabetical order, the once rehearsed regions
of here and there.
                   The very moment
she asks you to trace, outside of earthtime and watchtick, the slow
wearing away of the deer bone and hoof she has left
on your kitchen table, your ear
                            cups the wind,
committing to memory the steady
percussion of the leaves reminding you there is
nothing pinning you to this earth
but the gravity of love.

    Even now as you toss your head back laughing,
you see the difficulty of locating yourself
inside and outside the object of study:
                                    it's impossible not to view
the moon rising as an exhalation of the trees
that's part of another river.
                            You rise,
knowing there's not a verb that can hold you
there above the black openwork of the branches
where you have become the shape
of her gazing on this world.

2.

It was never a question of ladders, of measured distances.
Consider how you must tuck what's left
of your body under the fern,
     cool ribs and spine that go light and
dark, counting their way up your back. Green.
Where you crouched as a child.

No matter that it's winter, that the fern
is merely the idea of tendril,
       a delicate fixture
in the woods under snow, spore dust

     invisibly scattered. This close to earth
your anxiety about speechlessness falters:

look at the woman inside, bending over her desk
as if her cheek were weighted with stone
or the telling of it.
      Climb into the pine
outside her window, wait until her gaze lingers
on that fluctuating point of light among the cloistered branches:

   from that deep inside she must admit to her heart
the soluble blue of late afternoon light on snow
as the temporary phenomenon
it is.
   Do you think prayers rise?
          They're as lateral
as snow until wind lifts it up,
and this voice you hear, God knows, a meditation
on the reversible beauty of this world, its mineral
assault on the senses,
     the way the body
of the linden moistens the dark, companion to your longing
and refreshment those long summer nights.

It refuses to participate in the privacy of your despair;
it hasn't an inkling of doubt.
                              Not a leaf now,
not a shred of green. Snowbound.
And still you are flowing.

The Rain Carries on Its Back the Grief of Horses

cut off at mid-canyon, dust clapped
from the pilgrim's sandals circling the temple at Borobodur;
your mother's face, fragrance of red cedar, white phlox;
all the burdens the wind
cannot carry.   Because this isn't
enough, the rain also carries the sadness of miners,
the baptism of wolf-spider and vole; the names of the dead
a continent away; my sister's voice; the answers to all the ancient
texts pouring down the throat of the world; earth's antiphon: dust
and ash, song of the tin roof, the rungs to Jacob's ladder
dissolving.   Even as you sleep
the rain carries the trout's flesh, spare
hymnody of moss and rock, the drunken ghost
of Li Po and more: the dry riverbed calling from pole to pole
in the language of pelican and crow, blue egret and tern;
the futility of dustcloth and broom, obsolescence of fountain pen,
lead pencil, the painter's brush washed away,
all of it: their names, these losses,
that love.   Imagine
how the shoulders of the rain lighten
their load, letting go of longitudes and latitudes,
their sorrow and joy. How the spine of the rain — invisible,
shining — crumbles and loosens, dances and dissolves
into the moist syllables of the leaves; renews
the hidden narrative of cisterns, wells,
underground springs.   Surely
the rain shed for you carries on its back
the words you aren't able to say, all that silence splashing
and leaping, falling onto your hair now, washing
over eyebrow and lid like the tears
of the newly made.

Introit

Even if the scattering of leaves in the mind, the spiral
        descent of honey locust and ash,
                are useless hosannas,

If the dictations of the wind released as earth's
        address to the skin are kyries
                held in the flesh, whether

or not the spindles of rain falling all night
        on the heart, that washing and forgetting,
                are the *Agnus Dei's* of someone else's dream

offered up, still it would be foolish
        to empty yourself of that voice humming
                inside you like bees

crowding the field, even when it's empty.
        The boy scratching the dirt holds a prayer stick
                in his hands, the turning and lifting up

of dust a small matter of bliss; each leaf
        in the sugar maple's a door I want to walk through,
                the sanctus of every bird sings praise

for the boy stomping on the stick,
        for the cracking and breaking, the rise and fall.
                It's not the beginning or end of sorrow

that makes me want to dance in the dust,
        the leaves in my hair loosed by the wind, riddled
                by rain and these human feet,

dissolving beneath the pitch of the bees'
        abrasions, endurable
                simply by closing my eyes and singing.

Notes

"You Shall Be Weeping and Crying"
page 25 – The title, a translation from the German of the last line of the poem, is also the title of *Cantata #103* and its first movement for chorus.

"The Third Heaven"
page 40 – The title is taken from 2 *Corinthians* 12:2.

"Banishment of the Alleluia"
page 45 – The Banishment of the *Allelulia* is the first part of the liturgy for the Ash Wednesday service, during which the congregation says, "Enclose and seal up the word, alleluia. Let it remain in the secret of your heart, alleluia, until the appointed time."

"Why the Bee Does Not Fly into the Little Iron Pagoda in the Garden"
page 56 – St. Teresa of Avila wrote that "We will understand, when beginning to pray, that the bees are approaching and entering the beehive making honey"(from *Way of Perfection,* 28.7; trans. Kieran Kavanaugh). Her contemporary and great friend, St. John of the Cross, wrote the following lines while imprisoned by his own order in a tiny cell with a single high window, "How well I know that fountain's rushing flow/Although by night/Its deathless spring is hidden" (from *Song of the soul that is glad to know God by faith;* trans. Roy Campbell, *The Poems of St. John of the Cross).*

About the author

Kathleen Wakefield is the recipient of grants from the New York Foundation for the Arts and the Constance Saltonstall Foundation for the Arts. She has been a contributor to *The Georgia Review, Kenyon Review, The Journal,* and *Poetry.* She has taught poetry in schools in the Rochester area and at the Eastman School of Music. She lives in Penfield, New York, with her husband and their two sons.

The Anhinga Prize for Poetry Series

Notations on the Visible World
Kathleen Wakefield, 1999

Practicing for Heaven
Julia B. Levine, 1998

Conversations During Sleep
Michele Wolf, 1997

Man Under a Pear Tree
Keith Ratzlaff, 1996

Easter Vigil
Ann Neelon, 1995

Mass for the Grace of a Happy Death
Frank X. Gaspar, 1994

The Physicist at the Mall
Janet Holmes, 1993

Hat Dancer Blue
Earl S. Braggs, 1992

Hands
Jean Monahan, 1991

*The Long Drive Home**
Nick Bozanic, 1989

Enough Light to See
Julianne Seeman, 1988

*Conversing with the Light**
Will Wells, 1987

*The Whistle Maker**
Robert Levy, 1986

*Perennials**
Judith Kitchen, 1985

The Hawk in the Backyard
Sherry Rind, 1984

Sorting Metaphors
Ricardo Pau-Llosa, 1983

Out of print